I0538380

Amanda Duling

A Field Guide for Not
Quitting Too Soon

Amanda Duling, M.S.
Founder, One Gear Short of Normal™

One Gear Short of Normal™

Disclaimer

This book is provided for informational and educational purposes only. It is not intended as medical advice, diagnosis, or treatment. The information contained herein does not replace consultation with a licensed physician, physical therapist, or other qualified healthcare professional.

Endurance sports and physical training carry inherent risks, including injury, illness, or other adverse outcomes. Readers are solely responsible for their own health, training decisions, and medical care. Always consult a qualified healthcare provider before beginning or modifying any exercise program, especially if you have existing medical conditions, injuries, or concerns.

The author and publisher disclaim any liability for injury, loss, or damages incurred as a result of the use or application of the information presented in this book.

Participation in any training activity is undertaken at the reader's own risk.

TABLE OF CONTENTS

WHY THIS BOOK EXISTS 06-09

HOW TO USE THIS BOOK 10-12

START HERE 13-14

CHAPTER 1
You're Not Behind. You're New. 15-21

CHAPTER 2
Eat Before You Cry. 22-26

CHAPTER 3
Everyone Here Looks Fit
(They're Not Thinking About You). 27-31

CHAPTER 4
Pain Is Not the Entry Fee. 32-36

CHAPTER 5
More Isn't Better When You're Already Tired. . . . 37-41

CHAPTER 6
Group Rides Are Not Personality Tests. 42-46

CHAPTER 7
Your Bike Is a Tool, Not a Judgment. 47-51

CHAPTER 8
You Don't Need Everything Yet. 52-56

CHAPTER 9
Chaos Is Normal on Race Day. 57-61

CHAPTER 10
If You're This Tired, Rest. 62-66

CHAPTER 11
Your Brain Is Lying (Lovingly). 67-71

CHAPTER 12
This Still Counts Even If It Was Hard. 72-76

PANIC INDEX 77-80

QUICK REASSURANCE PAGES 81-82

STATE-BASED CHAPTER FINDER 83-84

TEAR-OUT / BOOKMARK PAGE 85-86

THINGS I THOUGHT MEANT
I DIDN'T BELONG (BUT DIDN'T) 87

WHAT ACTUALLY HELPED ME STAY 88

IF YOU ARE STILL HERE 89

WHEN TO ACTUALLY STOP 90-91

ABOUT THE AUTHOR 92

REFERENCES 93-94

WHY THIS BOOK EXISTS

This isn't a training plan.
It's not motivation.
And it's definitely not here to make you tougher.

It exists because endurance sports have an onboarding problem.

Most people don't quit endurance sports during a workout.
They quit in the parking lot.
On the drive home.
Late at night while replaying everything that felt awkward, slow, or wrong.

They don't disappear on race day.
They don't disappear mid-workout.
They disappear in quiet moments — the ones no one posts about.
In the car.

Research consistently shows that 50–70% of people who start a new exercise program drop out within the first three to six months. Not because they lack physical capacity — but because early uncertainty, negative affect, and low self-efficacy compound before identity has time to stabilize.

In plain terms:

They leave before things feel normal.

Endurance culture tends to focus on training plans, metrics, and performance. It assumes you've already decided to be here. It assumes you've already chosen this identity.

Almost no one explains how to enter without bouncing off immediately.

When you're tired, underfueled, overstimulated, or new, your brain is not a reliable narrator. Fatigue and low energy availability distort mood, confidence, and decision-making. That's not a mindset problem — it's biology.

Translation:

Your brain gets dramatic when your body is depleted or overwhelmed.

On top of that, endurance sports drop beginners straight into:

- Public comparison
- Unspoken rules
- Jargon
- Pain you don't yet know how to interpret

- Communities that already feel established

That's a terrible onboarding system.

And when people quietly leave, the story they tell themselves is usually:

I guess this just isn't for me.

This book exists to interrupt that moment.
Not forever.
Not philosophically.
Just today.

It is not a training manual.
It is not motivation.
It is not a mindset program.

It is an on-ramp field guide for the moments when doubt is loud and judgment is distorted by fatigue.

You will not find hype here.
You will find structure.

You will not be told to push through everything.
You will be given tools to decide later — when you are rested and regulated.

You do not need to feel confident to continue.

You only need to delay permanent decisions made under temporary stress.

That is enough.

HOW TO USE THIS BOOK

You don't read this cover to cover.

You open it when:

- You're sitting in your car before training and everyone looks fitter than you
- Your stomach feels weird and you're wondering if that's a sign
- Your bike is already racked and you're replaying everything that went wrong
- You're exhausted and suddenly convinced you should quit quietly

This book is meant to be used **in the moment**, when your nervous system is loud and your thinking is narrow.

Each chapter is short on purpose.
Each one follows the same rhythm on purpose.

You'll see:

- What's happening
- Why it's happening
- What's normal vs what actually needs attention
- And what to do right now

That structure isn't aesthetic. It's functional.

When people are stressed or depleted, they don't need more information — they need **clarity**. Clear, repeatable guidance reduces cognitive load and helps people make better short-term decisions under stress (Walsh et al., 2021).

So here's how to use this:

- Read one chapter. Or half of one.
- Stop as soon as you feel calmer.
- Do the next small thing.
- Decide nothing permanent while tired.

You can come back later.
You can reread the same page a hundred times. That's normal.

This book lives in:

- Your car
- Your gym bag
- The quiet space right before you almost talk yourself out of going

And one more thing, because this matters:

You are allowed to leave a workout early.
You are allowed to modify.
You are allowed to rest.

What I'm asking you *not* to do is quit from the car.

Decide later.
Decide rested.
Decide fed.

This book is here to help you stay long enough to make a real decision — not a panicked one.

That's it.

START HERE

If you are unsure where to begin, use this page.

If you feel:

- Like quitting from the car
  → Go to Chapter 1
- Like everyone else knows what they're doing
  → Go to Chapter 2
- Confused about pain or soreness
  → Go to Chapter 3
- Like a burden in a group
  → Go to Chapter 4
- Like doing more will fix everything
  → Go to Chapter 5
- Unsafe in a group environment
  → Go to Chapter 6
- Like being last means failure
  → Go to Chapter 7
- Guilty for resting
  → Go to Chapter 8
- Like you're behind everyone else
  → Go to Chapter 9
- Like this sport is an identity test
  → Go to Chapter 10

You do not need to read this book in order.

You need to read the section that matches your current state.

CHAPTER 1

You're Not Behind. You're New.

Name the Moment

You're sitting in your car.

You haven't opened the door yet, but your brain is already loud.

Everyone looks fitter.
Everyone looks like they know what they're doing.
Everyone looks like they belong.

You're doing the math in your head:

- How long you can pretend to check your phone
- Whether anyone noticed you park
- How fast you could leave without it being obvious

Here's the thing I want you to hear clearly, before your thoughts get any louder:

Nothing has gone wrong yet.

This feeling — the tight chest, the buzzing, the *why did I think this was a good idea* spiral — isn't a sign that you don't belong.

It's a sign that you're new **and you care.**

Those are not the same thing.

Why This Happens

Your brain is very good at protecting you from embarrassment, pain, and uncertainty.

When you're new, everything feels public:

- Your body
- Your pace
- Your gear
- Your breathing

Add fatigue, poor sleep, or low fuel, and your threat system turns the volume way up.

Research shows that when people are physically depleted, confidence drops and negative self-talk increases — not because anything is wrong, but because the brain is under-resourced (Matsui et al., 2011; Walsh et al., 2021).

Translation:
Your brain is not a reliable narrator right now.

The people you're comparing yourself to had this moment too.
They just don't remember it anymore.

Belonging doesn't arrive with confidence.
It arrives with repetition.

Normal vs Red Flag

Normal	Red Flag
• Feeling awkward or out of place • Wanting to leave before you start • Thinking everyone else is watching you • Doubting yourself when you're new	• Chest pain • Dizziness or faintness • Severe shortness of breath • Pain that escalates instead of easing

Feeling uncomfortable is expected.
Feeling unsafe is not.

What to Do Right Now

- Put your shoes on
- Take one slow breath that reaches your belly
- Eat something if you haven't
- Start slower than your ego wants

Your only job right now is to **open the door.**

You don't need to crush the workout.
You don't need to prove anything.

You can decide how you feel about this later.

Not from the car.

Truth to Keep

You don't have to feel confident to belong.
Confidence comes after you show up, not before.

Don't quit from the car.

CHAPTER 2

Eat Before You Cry.

Name the Moment

You're emotional.

Everything feels heavier than it should.
Your thoughts are dramatic.
You're either on the verge of tears or irrationally angry.

You're wondering:
Is this a sign I'm not cut out for this?

Before we spiral, let me ask you one very boring question:

Did you eat?

Why This Happens

Underfueling is one of the fastest ways people convince themselves endurance sports "aren't for them."

When blood glucose drops, mood, confidence, and decision-making go with it. That's not weakness. That's physiology (Thomas et al., 2016).

During longer or harder efforts, the brain can even run low on glycogen, which is strongly linked to emotional volatility and cognitive fog (Matsui et al., 2011).

This is why everything feels personal when you're depleted.

Hungry brains are mean brains.

Normal vs Red Flag

Normal	Red Flag
• Feeling shaky, irritable, or flat • Sudden self-doubt • Wanting to quit everything	• Confusion • Fainting • Persistent nausea or vomiting • Symptoms that don't improve after fueling

Bonking is not a personality trait.
It's a solvable problem.

What to Do Right Now

- Eat something with carbs
- Liquid calories count
- Drink fluids
- Sit for five minutes

Do not analyze your life while underfueled.

Feed first.
Decide later.

Truth to Keep

If you're crying and hungry, you're not having a personal crisis.

You're having a fueling issue.

Eat. Then reassess.

CHAPTER 3

Everyone Here Looks Fit (They're Not Thinking About You).

Name the Moment

You walk past racks, mirrors, tight kits.

Everyone looks strong.
Everyone looks lean.
Everyone looks like they know what they're doing.

Your brain says:
I do not look like these people.

And suddenly this feels like a mistake.

Why This Happens

Humans are wired for social comparison — especially in unfamiliar groups.

But here's the part your brain leaves out:

Most people are far more concerned with themselves than with you.

Research on group exercise shows that perceived judgment is a much stronger barrier than actual judgment (Anderson et al., 2016).

You're not being evaluated.
You're being noticed far less than you think.

Normal vs Red Flag

Normal	Red Flag
• Comparing bodies or gear • Feeling self-conscious • Assuming others are judging you	• Unsafe group behavior • Pressure to exceed your limits • Disregard for safety

Fast does not mean safe.
Confidence does not equal competence.

What to Do Right Now

- Look for one friendly face
- Stand where you feel less exposed
- Sit at the back
- Leave early if needed

You do not owe anyone performance.

Truth to Keep

No one is watching you.

And if they are, they're not the people you need to impress.

You belong because you showed up.

CHAPTER 4

Pain Is Not the Entry Fee.

Name the Moment

Something hurts.

Not the normal "this is effort" feeling — something sharper, louder, or more distracting than you expected.

And now your brain is trying to solve it with a familiar rule:

Maybe this is just what it takes.

Maybe everyone else hurts like this.
Maybe this is the price of admission.
Maybe you just need to push through.

Pause.

Pain is not the entry fee.

Why This Happens

Endurance sports blur the line between discomfort and pain early on.

You're told:

- It's supposed to be hard
- Soreness is normal
- Everyone hurts

All of that is *partly* true — and dangerously incomplete.

Discomfort is information about effort.
Pain is information about risk.

New athletes often don't have enough experience yet to tell the difference, so they assume the safest thing to do is endure it quietly.

That's how small problems become big ones.
Learning to listen early is not weakness.
It's skill development.

Normal vs Red Flag

Normal	Red Flag
• Muscle fatigue that eases with warm-up • Mild soreness after new activity • Temporary tightness that improves with movement	• Sharp or stabbing pain • Pain that worsens as you continue • Chest pain or pressure • Dizziness or lightheadedness • Numbness or tingling

Discomfort asks for patience.
Red flags ask for attention.

What to Do Right Now

- Slow down
- Change position or intensity
- Stop if something feels wrong
- Make a note of where and when it started

You are allowed to adjust in *real time.*

You are allowed to stop without explaining yourself.

Stopping early is not failing.
It's collecting information.

Truth to Keep

Suffering is not proof of belonging.

Staying healthy long enough to learn is.

CHAPTER 5

More Isn't Better When You're Already Tired.

Name the Moment

You feel behind.

Behind where you thought you'd be.
Behind everyone else.
Behind the version of you who imagined this going better.

So your brain offers a solution:

Do more.

More miles.
More days.
More intensity.

Because surely effort will fix the feeling.

It won't.

Why This Happens

When you feel insecure early on, the instinct is often to compensate with volume.

You assume that if you train more, push harder, or stack extra sessions, you will quiet the doubt.

This is predictable.

In early stages of skill acquisition, low confidence often drives overcorrection. Instead of building consistency, you try to accelerate belonging.

But adaptation does not respond well to panic.

More is not always commitment.
Sometimes it is fear.

Training stacked on insecurity often leads to exhaustion, not confidence.

Normal vs Red Flag

Normal	Red Flag
• Feeling tired after training • Needing rest days • Having fluctuations in motivation	• Persistent exhaustion • Loss of enthusiasm • Trouble sleeping despite fatigue • Training feels hard every day

If everything feels hard, something is off.

What to Do Right Now

- Take a rest or easy day
- Eat more than you think you need
- Sleep
- Reduce volume before intensity

You do not need to "earn" rest.

Rest is part of the work.

Truth to Keep

Consistency beats intensity.

Every time.

CHAPTER 6

Group Rides Are Not Personality Tests.

Name the Moment

You're worried you're too slow.

Too awkward.
Too much work.
Too obvious.

You're afraid you'll be the reason everyone else has a bad day.

So you hover at the edge, unsure whether to join or quietly disappear.

This feels personal.

It's not.

Why This Happens

Group environments amplify self-consciousness, especially when you're new.

There are unspoken rules:

- Pacing
- Drafting
- Hand signals
- Etiquette

No one is born knowing them.

Feeling uncomfortable in a group doesn't mean you're bad at this.
It means you're learning.

Groups that make learning unsafe are the problem.
Not you.

Normal vs Red Flag

Normal	Red Flag
• Anxiety before group workouts • Hanging at the back • Leaving early	• Unsafe pacing • Pressure to exceed your limits • Mocking or dismissive behavior • Ignoring safety

Fast does not equal responsible.

What to Do Right Now

- Position yourself where you feel safest
- Communicate if you need to leave
- Choose smaller or beginner-friendly groups
- Ride your own effort

You are not obligated to suffer socially to belong athletically.

Truth to Keep

You don't owe anyone performance.

You owe yourself safety and learning.

CHAPTER 7

Your Bike Is a Tool, Not a Judgment.

Name the Moment

You look at your bike and immediately start comparing.

It's older.
It's louder.
It's not the same brand as everyone else's.

You notice the clean lines, deep wheels, matching kits — and suddenly your bike feels like it's telling a story about you.

It's not.

Your bike is not a moral statement.
It's a tool.

Why This Happens

Endurance sports are unusually visible.

Gear is public.
Bodies are public.
Experience is implied through equipment.

That makes it easy to believe that "better" gear equals "real" athlete.

It doesn't.

Fit, comfort, and safety matter far more than brand names or price tags. Most early frustration comes from bikes that don't fit well, not bikes that aren't fancy enough.

A quiet, comfortable bike that fits you will take you farther than a flashy one that doesn't.

Normal vs Red Flag

Normal	Red Flag
• Feeling self-conscious about your bike • Not knowing how everything works yet • Minor noises you don't understand	• Persistent pain or numbness • Brakes or shifting that don't function reliably • Loose parts or obvious mechanical issues

Embarrassment is optional.
Safety is not.

What to Do Right Now

- Check comfort first: saddle, reach, bars
- Ask one specific question at a bike shop
- Learn one small maintenance task
- Ignore anyone who makes gear feel like a hierarchy

You don't need upgrades yet.
You need understanding.

Truth to Keep

A bike that fits and functions is a good bike.

Everything else is noise.

CHAPTER 8

You Don't Need Everything Yet.

Name the Moment

You start thinking about what you're missing.

Different shoes.
Different shorts.
Different helmet.
Different everything.

It feels like everyone else has a secret checklist you didn't get.

So you assume the problem is that you're under-equipped.

It probably isn't.

Why This Happens

Endurance sports are very good at selling solutions before you understand the problem.

Discomfort, insecurity, or confusion get misdiagnosed as a gear issue.

Sometimes gear *does* matter.
Most of the time, timing matters more.

Buying everything at once creates overwhelm, not confidence.

Learning what *actually* helps takes time — and experience.

Normal vs Red Flag

Normal	Red Flag
• Feeling tempted by gear upgrades • Wondering if equipment is holding you back • Feeling behind because others have more	• Buying gear to avoid training • Using purchases to quiet anxiety • Ignoring discomfort while shopping for upgrades

Gear should solve problems — not create pressure.

What to Do Right Now

- Identify one real issue
- Solve that issue only
- Delay purchases you don't fully understand
- Borrow or rent when possible

You're allowed to grow into this.

Nothing is urgent yet.

Truth to Keep

Buying less early is a skill.

You're learning it now.

CHAPTER 9

Chaos Is Normal on Race Day.

Name the Moment

Something goes wrong.

You forget something.
Your setup feels off.
The timing isn't what you expected.

You immediately think:
I wasn't ready.

Here's the reality:

Race day is a logistics event disguised as a fitness test.

Why This Happens

Races combine:

- Unfamiliar environments
- Time pressure
- Noise
- Nerves

Even experienced athletes miss things.

Chaos doesn't mean failure.
It means you're human.

The goal is not perfection.
It's adaptability.

Normal vs Red Flag

Normal	Red Flag
• Forgetting small items • Feeling flustered • Equipment not feeling "right"	• Unsafe equipment • Medical symptoms • Missing required safety gear

Nerves are expected.
Risk is not.

What to Do Right Now

- Pause before reacting
- Fix what actually matters
- Let go of what doesn't
- Use a simple checklist next time

Calm is a skill.
You can practice it.

Truth to Keep

One imperfect race does not define you.

Staying calm is a performance skill.

CHAPTER 10

If You're This Tired, Rest.

Name the Moment

You're exhausted.

Not the satisfying, *I worked hard* tired — the kind where everything feels heavier than it should.

Your legs feel flat.
Your motivation is gone.
Even easy things feel hard.

And now there's guilt layered on top of the fatigue.

You start wondering if you're just bad at this.

You're not.

Why This Happens

Endurance sports reward consistency, not constant intensity.

But early on, many people believe rest is something you earn — not something you need.

Fatigue accumulates quietly:

- Poor sleep
- Underfueling
- Stress
- Life

When recovery falls behind training, the body doesn't adapt — it resists.

Persistent fatigue isn't a motivation problem.
It's a recovery signal.

Normal vs Red Flag

Normal	Red Flag
• Feeling tired after harder efforts • Needing lighter days • Fluctuating energy	• Exhaustion that doesn't improve • Trouble sleeping despite fatigue • Loss of enjoyment • Getting sick repeatedly

Rest doesn't mean you're failing.

It means your body is asking for support.

What to Do Right Now

- Take a rest or very easy day
- Eat enough — especially carbs
- Prioritize sleep
- Reduce volume before intensity

Rest is not a reward.

It's part of the system.

Truth to Keep

Durability keeps you in the sport longer than toughness ever will.

Rest is how you stay.

CHAPTER 11

Your Brain Is Lying (Lovingly).

Name the Moment

You finish a workout and immediately start spiraling.

Everything feels wrong.
You replay mistakes.
You question why you're doing this at all.

Your brain starts offering dramatic conclusions:

Maybe I should stop.
Maybe this isn't for me.
Maybe everyone else is better.

This is familiar.

And temporary.

Why This Happens

Fatigue narrows perspective.

When you're tired, underfueled, or overstimulated, your brain prioritizes threat over accuracy.

That means:

- Negative thoughts get louder
- Confidence disappears
- Everything feels personal

This isn't insight.

It's biology.

Your brain is trying to protect you by convincing you to stop.

Normal vs Red Flag

Normal	Red Flag
• Harsh self-talk after effort • Wanting to quit immediately • Feeling emotional or flat	• Persistent low mood • Thoughts that don't lift with rest • Loss of interest beyond training

Most post-workout spirals resolve with food, rest, and time.

What to Do Right Now

- Eat something
- Drink fluids
- Sit quietly for a few minutes
- Delay all conclusions

Make a rule:
You don't decide anything permanent while depleted.

Truth to Keep

Your thoughts are information — not instructions.

Decide later.
Decide rested.

CHAPTER 12

This Still Counts Even If It Was Hard.

Name the Moment

It didn't go the way you hoped.

You finished — or you didn't.
It felt harder than expected.
You're not sure how to feel about it.

There's disappointment sitting next to relief.

And you're wondering if this even counts.

It does.

Why This Happens

Endurance culture celebrates outcomes:

- Distance
- Pace
- Podiums

But progress is built on exposure, not perfection.

Hard days teach your body and your brain what to expect next time.

Avoiding hard experiences doesn't build confidence. Surviving them does.

Normal vs Red Flag

Normal	Red Flag
• Mixed emotions • Wanting it to have gone better • Needing time to process	• Beating yourself up relentlessly • Dismissing effort entirely • Using one day to rewrite your story

One day is data — not a verdict.

What to Do Right Now

- Acknowledge what you did do
- Hydrate and eat
- Write down one thing you learned
- Let the day end

Reflection comes later.

Truth to Keep

Hard does not mean wrong.

If you showed up, this counted.

And if you're reading this right now, you didn't disappear.

That matters.

PANIC INDEX

If this is happening in your head, turn here.

You don't need to read explanations right now. You don't need to figure anything out.

You just need the right page.

This index exists so you can **flip faster than your brain can spiral.**

A

"Am I the slowest one here?" → Chapter 3
"Am I doing this wrong?" → Chapter 1
"Am I even cut out for this?" → Chapter 1, Chapter 11

B

Bike feels embarrassing → Chapter 7
Bike is making noises → Chapter 7
Body comparison spiral → Chapter 3
Bonked / shaky / emotional → Chapter 2

C

Chest feels weird → Chapter 4
Cried in my car → Chapter 2, Chapter 11
Confidence disappeared → Chapter 1

D

Didn't finish / had to stop → Chapter 12
Don't belong feeling → Chapter 1
Don't want to come back → Chapter 11

E

Everyone looks fitter than me → Chapter 3
Exhausted all the time → Chapter 10

F

Feel behind → Chapter 5
Feel judged → Chapter 3
Feel like quitting → Chapter 11

G

Group ride anxiety → Chapter 6
Gear envy → Chapter 8

H

Harder than expected → Chapter 12
Hurts more than it should → Chapter 4

I

I'm too old for this → Chapter 1
I should be better by now → Chapter 5

L

Left early / bailed → Chapter 6, Chapter 12

M

Motivation is gone → Chapter 10
Mixed feelings → Chapter 12

N

New and overwhelmed → Chapter 1
Nervous before starting → Chapter 1

P

Pain vs discomfort confusion → Chapter 4

Post-workout spiral → Chapter 11

R

Race day chaos → Chapter 9
Rest guilt → Chapter 10

S

Slow pace shame → Chapter 3
Stomach issues → Chapter 2

T

Too tired to train → Chapter 10
Training feels hard every day → Chapter 5

W

Want to quit right now → Chapter 11

If you didn't find the exact words you were looking for, flip to **Chapter 11.**

It's usually the right place.

QUICK REASSURANCE PAGES

(These pages are meant to be reread. Nothing new here. That's intentional.)

Things That Are Still True (Even When Your Brain Is Loud)

You don't have to feel confident to belong.
You're allowed to be new.
Awkward is part of the process.
Hard does not mean wrong.
Slow is still participation.
Rest is not quitting.
Pain is not the entry fee.
Bonking is not a personality trait.
Your brain lies when you're tired.
You can decide later.
You do not need to decide forever today.

Read This Before You Leave

If you showed up, it counted.
If you tried, it counted.
If you learned something, it counted.

Most people quit in moments like this.

If you're holding this book right now, you didn't.

Drink something.
Eat something.
Sit for a minute.

Don't quit from the car.

You can decide later.

STATE-BASED CHAPTER FINDER

If you don't know what you need, start here.

You don't have to name the problem perfectly. Just find the feeling that's closest.

If you feel...

- **Anxious before starting**
  → Chapter 1: *You're Not Behind. You're New.*
- **Emotional, shaky, or on edge**
  → Chapter 2: *Eat Before You Cry.*
- **Small, judged, or out of place**
  → Chapter 3: *Everyone Here Looks Fit (They're Not Thinking About You).*
- **Hurt, scared, or unsure if pain is normal**
  → Chapter 4: *Pain Is Not the Entry Fee.*
- **Behind, guilty, or like you're not doing enough**
  → Chapter 5: *More Isn't Better When You're Already Tired.*

- **Nervous about group rides or being "too slow"**
  → Chapter 6: *Group Rides Are Not Personality Tests.*
- **Embarrassed by your bike or gear**
  → Chapter 7: *Your Bike Is a Tool, Not a Judgment.*
- **Convinced you need to buy something to belong**
  → Chapter 8: *You Don't Need Everything Yet.*
- **Flustered or overwhelmed on race day**
  → Chapter 9: *Chaos Is Normal on Race Day.*
- **Exhausted and guilty about resting**
  → Chapter 10: *If You're This Tired, Rest.*
- **Spiraling after a workout or ready to quit**
  → Chapter 11: *Your Brain Is Lying (Lovingly).*
- **Unsure if what you did even counted**
  → Chapter 12: *This Still Counts Even If It Was Hard.*

If nothing here fits, turn to **Chapter 11.** It usually does.

TEAR-OUT / BOOKMARK PAGE

> # *Read This Before You Decide Anything.*

Nothing needs to be decided right now.
Eat something.
Drink something.
Sit down.

You are not allowed to judge your entire future while:

- Tired
- Hungry
- Emotional
- Or new

This moment is not a verdict.
It's a state.

You can leave early.
You can go slower.
You can try again another day.

Just don't quit from the car.

Decide later.
Decide rested.

(This page is meant to be folded, bookmarked, or kept somewhere obvious. If it looks worn, good.)

THINGS I THOUGHT MEANT I DIDN'T BELONG (BUT DIDN'T)

(Write anything. Single words count.)

-
-
-
-
-

(Nothing on this page disqualifies you.)

WHAT ACTUALLY HELPED ME STAY

(Write anything. Single words count.)

-
-
-
-
-

(You only need a few things.)

If you're reading this in your car, you're exactly where this book is meant to be used.

IF YOU ARE STILL HERE

If you have read this far, you have already done something most people do not.

You did not disappear quietly.

You paused.

You gathered information.

You delayed a permanent decision made in a temporary emotional state.

Endurance sports are not tests of identity.

They are repeated exposures to uncertainty.

Belonging does not arrive first.

It accumulates.

You do not need to feel certain to continue.

You only need to remain curious long enough to decide from steadiness instead of fear.

That is enough.

WHEN TO ACTUALLY STOP

This book encourages you not to make permanent decisions while tired.

That does not mean you ignore legitimate warning signs.

There are times when stopping — or pausing — is appropriate.

Seek medical evaluation if you experience:

- Sharp, stabbing, or worsening localized pain
- Swelling, instability, or joint locking
- Chest pain, dizziness, or shortness of breath beyond normal exertion
- Pain that changes your gait or movement pattern
- Symptoms that persist or worsen despite rest

Take a structured break if you notice:

- Persistent sleep disruption
- Loss of appetite
- Emotional volatility that does not resolve with rest

- Dread before every session
- Fatigue that does not improve with recovery

Stopping to gather information is not quitting.

Long-term participation requires health.

There is a difference between discomfort that builds capacity and pain that signals risk.

Learning that difference is part of becoming durable.

ABOUT THE AUTHOR

Amanda Duling is an endurance cyclist, post-bariatric athlete, and the writer behind *One Gear Short of Normal*™. She blends lived experience, evidence-based research, and dark humor to talk about the things athletes are told to endure quietly — and shouldn't.

She writes for athletes who almost quit.

REFERENCES

American Heart Association. (2024). *Warning signs of a heart attack.*

Anderson, P. J., et al. (2016). Social support and endurance exercise participation. *Journal of Obesity.*

Bicycling. (2025). *Bike fit basics and comfort adjustments.*

Farrance, C., et al. (2016). Adherence to group exercise interventions. *Preventive Medicine.*

IRONMAN. (2025). *Race-day logistics and transition planning.*

Matsui, T., Soya, S., Okamoto, M., Ichitani, Y., Kawanaka, K., & Soya, H. (2011). Brain glycogen decreases during prolonged exhaustive exercise. *Journal of Physiology, 589(13), 3383–3393.*

Meeusen, R., et al. (2013). Prevention, diagnosis, and treatment of overtraining syndrome. *Medicine & Science in Sports & Exercise.*

Thomas, D. T., et al. (2016). Nutrition and athletic performance. *Journal of the Academy of Nutrition and Dietetics.*

Walsh, N. P., Halson, S. L., Sargent, C., et al. (2021). Sleep and the athlete: Narrative review and expert consensus recommendations. *British Journal of Sports Medicine, 55(7), 356–368.*